Cosmos Cantata

A Seeker's Cosmic Journey

Tae-Sang Lee

Mayhaven Publishing, Inc.
P O Box 557
Mahomet, IL 61853
USA

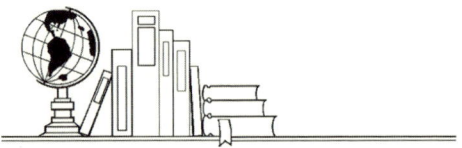

Cover Photograph: Cullen J. Porter
Copyright © 2013 Tae-Sang Lee
Library of Congress Control Number: 2013939481
First Edition—First Printing 2013
ISBN 13 978 1932278965
ISBN 10 1932278966

This little book is dedicated to
My grandsons Elijah and Theodore.
I feel really 'grand'
To encourage the enthusiasms
Children have,
To enhance their lion-hearts.

Table of Contents

Foreword — To Our Inner Child...7

Part One: Solo — Heartache Trickling Into the Sea of Cosmos
    1: Boy Who Loved Cosmos...13
    2: Cosmos Love-Song...17
    3: Self-finding — Life-Exploring...26

Part Two Duet-Trio-Quartet etc. — Heart-Song
    4: How to Love a Flower...33
    5: Where There's a Human, There's a Garden...38
    6: Sink or Swim...44

Part Three: Chorus — Miracle of Inevitability
    7: Watching the Night-Sea, Stars and Flowers...51
    8: What Two Cherries Symbolize...55
    9: Goldfish in a Bowl...60
    10: I Accuse the Old Generation of Panderism...66
    11: Cosmos in Dewdrops...69
    12: Happy That I Loved Cosmos...73

Part Four: Solo Again — May My Heart be the Sea of Cosmos!
    13: Cosmic Sound of Child-Song...77
    14: A Collapsed Bachelor-Tower...80
    15: Unexpected Opportunity...82
    16: Everything is a Miracle...85
    17: Postnatal Education — Name...88
    18: Our Self-Portrait — Froglike...96

Afterword: All's Wondrous Serendipity...99

"With our thoughts we make the world."

—Buddha

Tae-Sang Lee

The author Tae-Sang Lee
at home in his study

Foreword — To Our Inner Child

Soon after 9/11 a full-page ad in *The New York Times* displayed the photo of a person, along with his date of birth and death, followed by a short quote: "Enjoy the Game." It must have been friendly advice from the deceased to the living.

Harold and the Purple Crayon, a children's picture book by Crockett Johnson, is the story of a boy exploring the world of his imagination. It's a world where whatever he draws becomes reality, a world that is only a big playground for him. As for the child still alive in us, we too can become part of Harold's world, making it our favorite quote from Eleanor Roosevelt: "The future belongs to those who believe in the beauty of their dreams."

The Roman statesman Cicero (100 - 43 BC) purportedly declared people grew old not by aging but by forsaking idealism. So for the hope of the future he made the point, "Not to know what happened before one was born is always to be a child." Even then, as Johann Wolfgang Goethe observed, "No one is willing to believe that adults too, like children, wander about this earth in a daze and, like children, do not know where they come from or where they are going. . . .” Maybe, as Lao-Tzu says, “All are clear, I alone am clouded.”

We can only wonder that we were born yesterday as children; we are playing with our children today; and we will leave as children again tomorrow, baby-sitting our children's children.

Therefore, where there's a human, there's a garden as well.

Were there one saying to live by, methinks, or rather, mebe-lieves, it's Buddha's: “With our thoughts we make the world.” We are not only what we eat but also what we see, hear, read, think, imagine, dream and believe. Our eyes looking at flowers become flowers; our hearts yearning for stars become stars; and ‘I’ become ‘you’ as much as I like you. The great German mystic Jakob Boehme (1575-1624) believed that eternity consisted of a flash of a lightning-like moment when we became the very object of our love. Furthermore, we can never love anything or anybody enough.

Quantum mechanics claims that no distinction exists between time and space and that there is no past, present or future. New-tonian physics says it's possible to see light from a star that burned out a very long time ago, many light years away. Human bodies and stars are said to consist of the same basic elements. According to astrophotographers, new stars, just born, look like baby stars in the cradle, and the funeral of a huge star has the image of a butterfly flittering away. As the singer Joni Mitchell put it, “We are stardust,” and as the 1970s rockers sang, “All we are is dust in the wind.” If we came from a star and will fly home to a star, like Antoine de Saint-Exupery's *The Little Prince*, we should explore the sky, seeking to soar as high as we can, like *The Lark Ascending* by Ralph Vaughan Williams, ascending like Richard Bach's *Jonathan Livingston Seagull,* instead of imprisoning ourselves on earth. We live and we learn to fly.

I, too, believe the child in us is the divine 'god-ling'. Didn't Jesus say we couldn't enter heaven unless we were childlike? To a child, nothing is true or false, good or bad, beautiful or ugly, right or wrong, high or low, male or female; you and I are not separate, not separate from animals, plants or rocks. For, literally, all things in Nature are one and the same.

Most novels are autobiographical, and all autobiographies are novel-like. "Anything processed by memory is fiction, as is any memory shaped into literature," as the saying goes. Nevertheless, this is a story written down by an innocent, forever-young soul seeking the path to life and love as lived and loved by him. This is all for the purpose of transforming the prosaic side of life back into the sublime poetry — a child, that is.

—Tae-Sang Lee, on my 76th Birthday, December 30, 2012
Palisades Park, New Jersey U.S.A.

"There are only two ways to live your life.
One is as though nothing is a miracle.
The other is as though everything is a miracle."
—Albert Einstein

Part One — Solo
Heartache Trickling Into the Sea of Cosmos

1 Boy Who Loved Cosmos

2 Cosmos Love-Song

3 Self-finding — Life-Exploring

Boy Who Loved Cosmos

Boy was not aware that scraps of the moon and shooting stars were falling onto the bushes on the hill. Nor did he know that where they fell, the cosmos emerged.

The moon arose in the night sky. Boy, whose father died when Boy was five years old, looked at the hill his father had walked over. The wind blowing as always, the moon floating as usual, and the stars twinkling across the night sky, all came into view. Finding something, all of a sudden, that you have never seen before, was magical.

Boy stood up and started walking toward the hill, as his father had done a long time ago. Night fog seeped through the grass. It made him think of his favorite book. Boy could recite the whole story of *The Little Prince*, but he uttered the words he liked best: "In the face of an overpowering mystery, you don't dare to disobey."

The moon shone above him, and as he took a step he could see the stars moving, the moon growing bigger.

"Hi," a child greeted Boy when he reached the top of the hill.

"Hi," Boy said. Then the child raised his hand to his mouth to suppress a giggle.

"Why do you laugh?" Boy asked.

Trying to control himself, the child said, "Sorry. You look like a ghost, making me laugh. I'm really sorry."

Boy remained silent and then, looking up at the night sky, said, "It's strange tonight. The moon's growing larger, the stars are shaking and like a ghost Father is appearing. It never happened like this."

The child nodded. "There are thirty ghosts in every living being."

"What, what do you mean?"

"That's because the ratio between the dead and the living is thirty to one and from the beginning of the world about one trillion people have lived on the planet Earth."

"Who, who said so?"

"Who else? Someone who lived on Earth said so."

"Who, who's that?"

"The name is Arthur Clarke. Do you know him?"

"No, no. I don't know him."

After a pause, the child giggled again.

"Why do you keep laughing?"

"Don't you find the number interesting? About one trillion people have lived on Planet Earth and there are about one trillion stars in the Milky Way."

"Is, is that true?"

"Yes, that means each one of us has a star of one's own."

Boy kept silent, looking up at the moon and stars.

Breaking the silence, the child asked, "Are you about to leave?"

"How did you know?"

"I just know."

"Why do the stars shake? Why does the moon grow bigger? It is about to explode."

Boy tried in vain to recall what his father looked like. He could not see his father's face as he watched him walking away toward the hill — and so he could not remember.

"I'm leaving. Goodbye!" Boy said to the child. And he started to walk away.

The child didn't say a word. He watched the moon expand and explode like fireworks, scattering fragments of the moon and shooting stars all over the bushes, but Boy was not aware of what was happening. Moreover, Boy didn't know that where the fragments fell the cosmos flowered.

Not long after, that Boy left home and went on a journey. People said Boy became a vagabond at an early age.

One summer night, Boy left a poem:

Jae-Sang Lee

Cosmos

When I was a boy,
I liked the cosmos
Cozy and coy
Without rhyme or reason to toss.

Later on as a young man
I fell in love with cosmos,
Conscious of the significance
Of this flower for me sure,
The symbol of a girl's love pure.

As I cut my wisdom teeth,
I took the cosmopolitan road
Traveling the world far and near
In my pursuit of cosmos in a chaotic world.

Upon looking back one day,
Forever longing, forever young,
Never aging and never exhausted
By yearning for cosmos,
I'd found unawares numerous cosmos
That had blossomed all along the road
That I had walked.

A dreamland of the bluebird
Looking for a rainbow,
Where could it be?
Over and beyond the stormy clouds
That's where it could be!

Cosmos Love-Song

"Call me a crazy, stupid madman, or what you may. I'll jump into the sea, into the bosom of the Cosmos." After sending this note off to Cosmos, Young Man threw himself into the East Sea.

Come autumn, wherever you go in the countryside of Korea, the pure and pretty cosmos, shyly swaying in the breeze, catches the wanderer's eye all along the journey. At times like this, you suffer from an old heartache.

As a constant stream of humanity flowed by, Boy became Young Man called Y.

One day in a bakery café, Y was instantly captivated by a girl so pure and pretty. It was love at first sight. If she were a flower, what flower would she be? There was a saying that among all the creations of God, the cosmos was the first and the chrysanthemum was the last. While Y was in a daze, she was leaving. He hesitated before following her.

She became aware of being followed from downtown Chongro to Sinchon on the outskirts of town. "Do you have any business with me?" she asked. She had a clear voice.

"Please let me introduce myself. I'm a new philosophy-religion graduate of Seoul National University. I want to make your acquaintance, if I may. Do you mind?"

She blushed scarlet. Y was delighted and decided to call her his Cosmos.

Y started dating his Cosmos, known as C. They frequented music cafés like C'est Si Bon, and The Milky Way, in downtown Seoul.

One day they went to see a film, *The Brothers Karamazov*. Waiting in the second-floor lobby for the next show-time, C asked, "Do you want to go to the bathroom?"

Y didn't feel like going, but he went anyway. The entrances to the men's and women's bathrooms were side by side. Y stood for a moment in front of the urinal and a thought crossed his mind that he and C were not far apart with only a wall between them. He realized if the distance was shortened by just a few feet, he could be in her. At the very moment he experienced the contraction of the space. Thereafter, he never felt lonesome again. Anytime, anywhere, he could feel close to anybody. If the whole universe were compressed into a single dot, one could be united with all.

In the meanwhile, a powerful opposition politician asked Y to become his secretary. Y's involvement with the student movement opposing the corrupt and dictatorial government must have caught his attention. Y declined the offer because he had other plans. In the future, be it politics, economics or culture, in all walks of life, he thought, it was going to be global, and therefore learning foreign languages was essential. Since middle and high school he'd been learning English, Japanese, Chinese, German, French and Spanish. And in college he studied Latin, Greek, Hebrew, Russian and Arabic. He became fluent enough in English, German, French and Spanish to tutor fellow students, businessmen and military generals.

Being a greenhorn at that age, Y decided three jobs were unworthy of a man: secretary, spokesperson and ghostwriter. If you possessed a modicum of self-respect, he reasoned, why should you run errands, speak for another or write for somebody? If you became a secretary, why not become a presidential secretary? Even that was not because he coveted the position of a presidential aide. There's an old saying in Korea: "You've got to enter a tiger's den if you want to catch a tiger." This was not to say he thought of harming anyone, but it was rumored that President Syngman Rhee, the first president of the Republic of Korea, was surrounded by a pack of sycophants and schemers blinding him to the true state of affairs. If Y worked for him, he would open up the President's eyes and ears to people's needs and problems. In fact, he had secured a glowing recommendation from a VIP for a protocol post of the Kyungmudae, the President's Office — now called the Blue House.

After graduating from the Kyungnam Girls' High School in Busan, C attended the School of Pharmacy, Ewha Women's University, in Seoul. Before going home for the winter break of 1959, C gave Y a copy of Dante's *The Divine Comedy* as a Christmas present. He was going to visit C and her parents in Busan as soon as he received his official appointment. In case he couldn't make it for some reason, he also made an appointment to see her on the next Valentine's Day at the Lake Restaurant in Seoul.

A few days later Y fled the capital. Because of the active part he played in the student movement, he had to go into hiding. After going underground, he wrote a letter to C. Writing in ink wouldn't convey the urgency and the intensity of his love for her, so he drew blood from his forearm and calligraphed the note in blood. Apologizing for not keeping the appointment, he begged for understanding and asked her to wait for him until he could contact her. His message to her was rolled into a parcel and mailed. Apparently frightened by this shocking 'blood-letter,' C replied with a short note saying, "Please forget me."

Falling into an abyss of despair, Y devised a plan on how to take his own life. If he could find a boat, he could row it as far as he could in that great expanse, the sea and the sky, often likened to a life-journey itself. If not, he would simply jump into the sea and swim as far as he could.

As if drawing a long-kept sword, Y wrote a suicide note:

Dear Cosmos,

Call me a crazy, stupid madman or what you may. I'm going to jump into the sea, into the bosom of the Cosmos.

After sending this parting note off, Y threw himself into the East Sea. Were life and death indeed providential? Y's one life was miraculously spared, escaping from ninety-nine deaths. In the hopeless turmoil, he hurt his back and was hospitalized. After his surgery at the Medical Center in Seoul, the simmering Student Uprising of April 19, 1960, finally erupted.

Reading newspapers one day, Y spotted someone identified as Cosmos on the list of donors helping the victims of the Uprising who were killed or wounded by the police. Y intuited that it was his Cosmos! She was grieving over Y's victimhood, for sure. He was deeply moved. Even if he were to breathe his last at that very moment, he could not have been happier. After one surgery Y recuperated, but he pretended otherwise and underwent two more surgeries. Following operations on his spine to remove herniated discs, he wished he would never have awakened from the anesthetic. But even if he came to himself, he would be happy with vivid memories of C forever.

Hospitalized for almost a year, thinking of C day and night, Y happened to read a newspaper article on graduating students of Ewha Women's University. C was a senior there. Asked about their personal views on marriage, a few students said they didn't want to get married at all.

21

One observation, in particular, was penetrating: "Man's life seems too tough and tragic." These words took away his breath and soul.

"Oh, my goodness, my Cosmos thought I was dead and couldn't forget me. And she wouldn't marry. What a horrible thing I've done to her. I've got to set her free from this nonsense."

Then Y panicked when he recalled hearing that someone became impotent after a spinal surgery. "Have I become impotent too? Even if not, could I father a child?" Y asked himself. He was apprehensive of his conditions. Only after his sperm was tested and he received a clean bill of health, did Y write to C for an appointment to meet her at the Lake Restaurant on the next Valentine's Day, February 14, 1961. He planned to get the two families together to arrange for the two young people's engagement.

Y went to C's school to check if she got his letter. The letter was still in the school mailbox — uncollected. He inquired C's whereabouts and went to deliver it himself.

In no time, after speaking with her, it dawned on Y that his was the typical case of "misconception at liberty and delusion at sea." C told Y that she was seeing another man. Thunderstruck by the harshness of reality, he wished her all the happiness.

That night, before weeping himself to sleep, Y wrote down a poem about walking on the beach after a thunderstorm:

The Sea

Thou
Symbolizing
Eternity, infinity and the absolute
Art
God.
How
Agonizing
A spectacle is life in blindness
Tumbled into Thy callous cart
To be such a dreamy sod!

A dreamland of the gull
Of sorrow and loneliness full
Where would it be?
Beyond mortal reach would it be?

May humanity be
A sea of compassion!
My heart itself be
A sea of communion!

I envy Thy heart
Containing
Passions of the sun
And
Fantasies of the sky.

I long for Thy bosom
Nursing
Childlike enthusiasm
And
All-embracing mother nature.

Although a drop of water,
It trickles into the sea.

Absurd and wild though it may have been, this poem expressed Y's instinctive prayer. Undoubtedly, this call of the sea made him seem like a precocious child. But alas, his desires remained child-like. Preoccupied with self-criticism, he was unable to be as natural or as divine as the sea. Was this fanciful vision a trace of childhood innocence or a vestige of human divinity? He would never know, though he should know as he had suffered so much for it. The words he used to address himself were now all charged with disparate meanings.

He could feel, welling up within himself, the scene evoking a long and enduring train of reminiscences. For him, he fancied, to love was to be born into cosmos. But alas, much too much to his chagrin, he couldn't love himself. He could love no one until and unless he could love himself.

Wasn't he hopelessly misdirected in the early days of his life when he was going to enlarge his life by emptying all the small things he belittled but of which life was composed? What a deed of derring-do!

24

Perhaps, though, he did not fail in perseverance of striving to live up to his name Haesim '해심' (in Korean), and '海心' (in Chinese), meaning 'Heart of the Sea.' In this light, maybe, he could stop loathing himself and start loving himself for being a wanderer, as a wise old Korean saying notes, "to perceive the whole of the universe through a blade of grass."

Perhaps, then, his sufferings were not in vain after all. Unwittingly he had come to discover his own unique identity he so anxiously longed to bring to light, not to find shame, but to cherish and to nourish.

From this fountainhead would spring his sense of decency and dignity he so despaired of ever feeling. From this wellspring would begin a pilgrimage of a little drop — be it a dewdrop or a raindrop — trickling into the sea of cosmos, with a few grains of sand or stars serving as his companions on the journey.

Self-Finding — Life-Exploring

God was driven out of Y's heart, and his 'blood-letter' frightened away his Cosmos. In their place a life filled with longing for someone, as yet unknown, slowly kindled.

"Amongst all the religions of the world, Christianity is the only true religion and the others are all superstitions," the most senior professor of the Religious Studies began his lecture with this statement. Y was confused. Weren't all religions concerned with believing in and worshiping a superhuman, controlling power or powers, providing standards of morality and achieving true happiness? Making such a statement to his students showed the professor to be completely irresponsible.

When Y entered college, he had tried to decide on his subject major. College education would civilize him. He would become a 'cultured' person. He expected nothing more. But he first needed to find a map and compass, for they were indispensable for the voyage. If life was really like a floating 'leaf-boat,' and if you'd like to sail as you wished, you would need to have a sense of direction, above all a philosophy of life. That's why Y chose philosophy and religion as his major subjects.

The professor continued the lecture, "Out of all the denominations, only the Methodists are orthodox, and all the others are heretic. . . . If there are one thousand Christians, only one of them is a true believer. . . "

Y stood up in protest, "Professor, please permit me to ask you a question. If one's faith is precious, wouldn't it be the same with others too?"

"What? What do you dare to mean by that?"

The professor was clearly angry.

Y lowered his voice, "Professor, I know well-behaved children do not answer back when scolded. However, I am just pointing up the necessity for caution and fair-mindedness, if I may. Listening to your self-righteous statements, I'm reminded of Mahatma Gandhi's remark that but for the Christians, we could all be Christians. If there were no Christianity, there would be no Crusade, Prof. . . "

Becoming impatient and growing more furious, the Professor yelled, "Go away, you Satan!"

Y left the classroom without saying another word, realizing that all attempts at counterargument would be futile.

In high school Y had been a fanatical churchgoer. For fear that his soul would be condemned to burn in hell for all eternity, he didn't go near a movie theater. But disappointed with the Church altogether, and filled with infinite curiosity, he determined to explore life itself.

Y started voraciously reading previously forbidden novels and watching forbidden movies. However, he was not satisfied with a vicarious thrill of the experience of others in a world of make-believe and fiction. He wanted to have first-hand experience of the characters in all the dramas. He desired to create 'true-stories' of his own life. From then on, he searched in deadly earnest for the love of his life. He thought it would be nice to find a girl well brought up and take good care of her. It would be nicer if he could meet somebody who had a hard life and make her happier. He even ventured into brothels and rescued some of the young sex slaves by paying off their debts. In so doing, his heart was broken repeatedly.

Then Y happened to read a short story that captured his imagination. It was a story of an American soldier serving overseas.

One day the soldier entered the military library where he found a copy of Somerset Maugham's *Of Human Bondage* among books donated by civilians back home.

As he was reading, the soldier was distracted by some interesting musings scribbled on the margin in a feminine hand that aroused his curiosity. He tried to find the writer and, after a long search, he obtained her name and address. Eventually they became pen pals.

When World War Two ended, the soldier was discharged. He and his pen pal arranged to meet at a train station platform. He arrived and looked around for the woman. Since each did not know what the other person looked like, he was carrying a copy of the novel and she was wearing a flower in her lapel — just as they told each other.

He found someone with a flower in her lapel. It turned out she was an elderly woman. For a second he was disappointed, and yet he greeted her, introducing himself with a big smile. Without pausing for breath, the old lady whispered something in his ear that sent him flying towards the beautiful young lady who was waiting for him at a nearby restaurant.

This story inspired Y to find an ideal life-mate. One such means would be a pen pal. In communicating by letter he was less likely to pre-characterize someone. By exchanging thoughts and feelings, he could get to someone in a relaxed nonjudgmental fashion, he thought.

After leaving the college lecture hall, Y abandoned the hereafter and God-oriented religion. His Cosmos had been frightened away by his 'blood letter.' He was filled with longing for someone as yet unknown.

Y always had an image of the perfect woman:

There is a Lady Sweet and Kind

There is a lady sweet and kind,
Was never a face so pleased my mind;
I did but see her passing by,
And yet I love her till I die.

—English poet Barnabe Googe (1540-94)

29

Y kept on reciting to himself what the masterful Persian poet Jalal ud-din Rumi (1207-73) wrote:

I would love to kiss you
(The price of kissing is my life)
Now my loving is running toward my life
Shouting: "What a bargain,
Let's buy it!"

Part Two

Duet-Trio-Quartet etc. —— Heart-Song

4 How to Love a Flower

5 Where There's a Human, There's a Garden

6 Sink or Swim

How to Love a Flower

"I should never have run away!" Y told himself. "Flowers are so contradictory. I should have known better that lots of love and affection were hidden behind her witticism — for surely flowers say so well what they don't mean. But I was too young to know how to love her."

The moon rose in the night sky. Y appeared near the top of the hill. The stars spread across the sky. He suddenly took notice of something he had not seen until that moment. The grass was wet with early morning dew. And every time Y took a step, stars were moving too.

"Hi, Uncle Y!"
When Y arrived at the very top of the hill, the child greeted Y as if he had been waiting for him.
"Hello. You still look the same."
Then the child covered his mouth, repressing a giggle.

"Why do you laugh?" Y asked.

"Uncle Y, you look like a ghost. I couldn't help it. I'm sorry."

"Wasn't I like that at all times? Not like a ghost, more like a beggar, I must say."

"Um, in truth, I'm afraid so," the child frankly admitted, and they both laughed.

When they stopped laughing, they fell silent. The moon grew bigger and the stars were moving. Presently, the child broke the silence, "Uncle Y, have you ever loved anyone?"

There was a moment of silence.

"Yes, I once loved the Cosmos. In floral language, the cosmos means a girl's love, pure and simple. Still, I thought that a flower, and her words, said so convincingly what she didn't really mean. But I don't know if love and affection were hidden behind her witticism. I haven't the slightest idea what went wrong. Was I too young to know how to love her?"

"Did you think she was one of a kind?"

"Yes, and I want to have a flower of my own, and yet I couldn't have this one. I want to know why."

"Maybe, Uncle, it's because there are many flowers."

The moon was up and the stars were shining. Y was inspired to tell a story. "Do you know there was a man born posthumously to a family that had only one child — each for three consecutive generations? This man fathered a dozen children and loved all children, not just his own. He published a children's book entitled *Children's Paradise*, a collection of poems, songs and plays he wrote for children. It was written in Korean when the Korean language was banned by the Japanese who occupied Korea for 35 years — until the end of World War II. Under the Japanese rule, Korean people lost not only their language and culture but also their names and identities when they were forced to give up their Korean names and adopt Japanese names, instead. As you may already know, the grown-ups are much more childish, silly and stupid than children. Of 500 copies printed, the one copy of *Children's Paradise* my father kept at home was lost during the war. I read the poem when I first learned to read. I do not remember the exact wording of one poem, "Goldfish," but I remember the essence of the poem. It was about a child talking to himself on a rainy day, looking at a goldfish in a bowl. Do you want to hear it?"

The child remained silent.

Y began reciting the poem.

Goldfish

Always happy at play swimming
Around and around
Gaily and merrily
You were,
My dear goldfish.

Why then are you so still today,
Not in motion at all?
What's the matter with you?
Maybe you're homesick,

Missing your Mom and Dad,
Your sisters and brothers,
All your dear friends,
Soaked with memories and thoughts of
Your home in the water-land
Far away, over yonder, of yore.

I do like you so very much.
I do want to live with you
Forever and ever in this house.
I don't want to lose you.
I don't want to part company from you.

I'll be very sad to be separated from you.
I'll be missing you so very much.
And yet I'll have to set you free.
I must let you go home.
Yes, my dearest goldfish,
I'll let you go back to your water-land
In the Han River.

It breaks my heart to see you looking so sad.
It hurts so very much.
I love you much too much
To keep you away from your folks.
I can't be happy if you are not happy.
I just want you to be happy.
That's all I wish.

When he finished the poem, Y was in contemplative mood. He thought aloud, "Perhaps because of the deep impression the poem made on me, I have lived my life with this philosophy of the gold-fish ever since. I was a child when I played with friends and if any-one wanted to quit playing, I stopped right away, even if I wanted to continue, because I always accepted whatever people said to me. My friends advised me not to take at face value what a girl said, not to take a no for an answer. They told me that a girl's 'no' means maybe and her 'maybe' means yes. I failed every time, however, by naively taking girls' words literally. The arrow has to fly straight and true to the target."

After a cautious silence, Y said rather abruptly, "I'll return."

The child responded as if he had expected Y's comment. "It may not be a good idea to go back to your childhood. It will be painful, breaking your heart all over again."

"I'll have to return to my childhood so that I can find the Cosmos," Y said, starting to walk away.

The child remained silent and stood on top of the hill while Y made his way back into his childhood.

Where There's a Human, There's a Garden

Even in the midst of a war, flowers bloomed. North Korean soldiers bought fruits and home-baked bread from Boy. South Korean soldiers gave him some of their daily rations. An older brother of his classmate paid for the entire stock of rice-candy Boy was peddling. A nursing officer gave him a large sum of money without taking anything from the wares he was selling. A grandfatherly owner of a grain-store paid a good price for an ox-cartload of rice Boy and his mother brought to his store. Their humanity blossomed in his heart.

Early in the summer of the year when Boy was a seventh grader, the war broke out. Like almost everyone else living in Seoul, Boy's family couldn't flee the capital city because the bridges over the Han River were destroyed.

Boy's father was born after his father had died. He was the only child of the family. So was Boy's grandfather and great-grandfather. Boy's father fathered twelve children, but he was taken

38

away when Boy was five.

Boy didn't grow up big in height — nor in his heart.

One day, despite his mother's urging that he should not go out, Boy left his home to see the city streets engulfed in flames following heavy artillery fire and bombings. Debris was everywhere. Walking along the streets, Boy stopped at the side of a collapsed building. In the middle of an untended garden overgrown with weeds, Boy discovered some flowers. They were cosmos in pink and red. Boy gasped with surprise at the cosmos blooming in the hot summer weather. Boy was used to seeing the cosmos in the fall. And then, out of the blue, there was a hailstorm. The hail ricocheted off a nearby wall, raising a cloud of dust on the ground. Boy instinctively crouched down. He soon realized the hail was machine-gun bullets from fighter jets flying low — just above the buildings. Moments later he raised his head. When he stood up, he saw bullet holes on the wall and looked at the pink cosmos in the grass. Had he not lain flat on the ground, he would have been hit by bullets.

Boy scoured the razed city streets, scampering around like a squirrel. According to his friends, the orchards on the outskirts of the city were strewn with fruit left by people who had fled. The orchards were not covered with fruit, but he found some, put them in a bag and dashed home.

When Boy was near home, he encountered North Korean soldiers. Fear made him freeze and he stopped dead in his tracks. One of them beckoned him over with a wave. Boy wanted to run away but his legs wouldn't move.

"What's in the bag?" the soldier asked.

"F. . . fruits. . . "

"Where did you get them?"

"G. . . G. . .Grandpa gave me."

"Fruits, did you say?"

Boy felt his death was sure, and the fruits would be taken away — for certain. He was on the verge of tears.

"Can you sell the fruits, or exchange them for rice?" The soldier lifted a bag of rice to show to Boy.

"All — all right. I can bring home-baked bread, if you like," Boy said, much relieved. He knew his mother often baked bread.

"This little comrade is a fine figure of a boy! Okay, if you bring enough bread for all of us, I'll give you two bagsful of rice."

The soldier smiled at Boy and Boy smiled back. When Boy returned with the bread, he was welcomed by the soldiers and rewarded with more rice.

Boy befriended the troops and acquired provisions for his family to tide over the hard times. Eventually the North Korean forces retreated from Seoul, and South Korean and American forces reentered the capital city. Boy continued his business of hawking whatever he could find to sell. South Korean soldiers gave him some of their daily rations. Meanwhile, winter withered all the cosmos.

"The North Korean troops are coming back, they say, and the Red Chinese Army too. We have to leave." Boy's words were uttered in gasps while his mother was busy packing. "Mother, you go ahead of me. I'll follow you."

"What are you talking about? You could be hurt."

Nevertheless, Boy persisted and stayed behind.

The North Korean and Red Chinese forces came. This time, they couldn't afford to buy anything from Boy. He walked all the way to the city of Daejon — nearly 100 miles away from Seoul, in the central part of the country — and joined his family. Everybody was without food, and his family was no better off.

Boy went hawking in the streets crowded with refugees. He started selling kimpab (sushi) that his mother made. It wasn't something special, but he had no problem feeding the hungry refugees. He then sold rice-candies in the waiting area and plaza of the railway station. Becoming a bit more venturesome, he jumped over the fence and sold candies at the platform and in the train cars. A steward spotted Boy and chased after him, shouting, "How you dare come on the train. . . "

When Boy jumped off the train, the steward raced after him. The train started moving slowly. Boy had no choice but to scurry between moving wheels, throwing himself across the rails. Luckily he didn't get hurt and he managed to lose his pursuer.

Because of the chaos that followed, Boy didn't have spare clothes and wore his school uniform and cap with his school badge. A man in military uniform stopped to ask Boy, "Did you go to Kyungbock Middle School?" He was a second lieutenant of the South Korean Army.

41

"Yes," Boy replied.

"Do you know Youngchol Kim?"

"Oh, Youngchol, you mean? He's a classmate of mine."

"Really? Youngchol is my younger brother."

"Is that right? My name is Haesim."

"I'm glad to meet you, my little friend."

The officer paused for a moment, then said, "Can you wrap up everything?"

"Do you mean all of these rice-candies?"

"Yes, all of them."

After paying Boy, the second lieutenant bade farewell, patting him on the head.

Another time, a female military nursing officer walked towards Boy and then halted. "You're having a hard time, aren't you?" she asked.

Boy blushed with embarrassment. People kept making eyes at this attractive woman in uniform. She was beautiful. He just smiled vaguely. Then she handed a large sum of money to Boy. His initial reaction was to decline to accept the money.

"It's all right. You can keep the money."

She put the money in his pocket. In return for her generous gift of money, the boy wrapped up everything he had and gave it to her. But his offer was waved aside.

"Now take care and goodbye!"

The nursing officer hurried away before the boy could do anything. Stunned, Boy stared blankly into space with a faraway look, not knowing whither she was gone.

It was in the middle of that winter of 1950 when Boy and his mother bought many sacks of rice and climbed aboard a freight train. They had heard the price of rice was much higher in the south where it was swarming with refugees. The freight train moved slowly. Though frozen and tired, they endured the week-long ordeal perched on a mound of rice sacks, braving the elements. They got off at the southern town of Gupo, in the South Kyungsang Province, and loaded an oxcart. When they called on a rice merchant, he complimented Boy on his enterprise and paid a good price for the load. They made a handsome profit.

They were relieved. Even in the midst of a war, flowers were blooming. The North Korean soldiers who bought Boy's wares, the South Korean soldiers who gave him part of their daily rations, the brother of his classmate who paid for all of his rice-candies, the nursing officer who handed him a good amount of money and the grandfatherly owner of a grain-store who took over the ox-cartload of rice from Boy — their humanity had blossomed into loving care.

Sink or Swim

Boy set up a small business in earnest in a flea market of the city. Displaying over 100 black-market items sold by American GIs trafficking in U.S. Army PX goods, Boy called aloud for attention to his goodies.

One day, Boy went to the area where the U.S. I Corps was stationed in order to replenish his stock of Yankee goods. When the boy got there, military equipment and personnel were being loaded onto trucks. The whole unit of troops was moving. The boy approached the officer sitting in a jeep at the head of a long line of vehicles. Since his English was limited, Boy managed to utter just a couple of words, "I your houseboy. OK?"

The officer looked at him intently and then motioned Boy to hop onto the backseat of his jeep. Boy said breathlessly, "Wait a moment. I must go and speak to Mother."

Smiling, the officer, with his big hands, lifted Boy and sat him in his front seat, saying something to his driver.

"Yes, sir."

"Where's your mother?"

Boy directed the driver, pointing towards the market. He told his mother that he was going away with the American troops.

From that day on, Boy was a diligent worker, shining shoes, making beds and running errands for officers and the rank and file. Though he was a child, he did not have to be told what to do.

Officers and enlisted men showered the boy with chewing gum, candies, cookies, chocolate. He took them to his mother whenever he visited her.

U.S. Army I Corps moved north beyond the 38th Parallel and then retreated back south to Seoul. When he finished his job early in the morning, Boy went to a school set up temporarily for the refugee-children in Seoul.

The commanding officer who took Boy as his houseboy was a colonel who loved classical music. Soon, Boy became a little classical music buff, too.

"If you'd like to study music, I'll send you to the Juilliard School in New York," the officer promised.

The commanding officer's tour of Korea would soon be over and he'd be returning to America. One evening the officer wanted to have a word with Boy.

"I'll be returning home shortly," he told Boy. "You know I've been treating you like my own son. If you decide to come with me to America, I'll adopt you and send you to an American school. What do you think about that?"

"Thank you, sir. But I have to ask my mother."

45

"Where is she now?"

"She's still in Daejon City."

"All right, then, go talk to your mom."

The next day Boy went to see her. As always, his mother was very happy to see him. He could not sleep and was not able to tell his mother an American officer wanted to take him to America and adopt him.

On his return, Boy said, "I'm sorry. Mother doesn't want me to go to America."

The officer dialed up the phone and talked to someone. After he hung up, he kissed Boy on his forehead and said, "I understand. Stay well in Korea."

On the morning of the day the officer was leaving for America, an American GI driver came to pick up Boy and take him somewhere. The officer put his hands on Boy's shoulders and said, "I've asked a good friend of mine to take good care of you. Goodbye, my boy."

The officer was in tears, but Boy did not cry. He did not want to show a sign of weakness.

Driven away in a jeep, Boy looked back. The officer was waving to Boy. When Boy looked back again, the officer had disappeared from sight. Then, and only then, did Boy burst into tears.

Much to his surprise, Boy was taken to Daejon City.

The commanding officer's friend was also a colonel in charge of the CAC, a United Nations organization for the reconstruction and rehabilitation of war-torn South Korea. Except for the colonel, all the other staff members were civilians representing the United Nations member countries participating in the Korean War. Their living quarters were located in the western suburb of the city. The colonel had a houseboy, but it just so happened that the houseboy of the deputy head of the organization stole something and ran away a couple of days before, so Boy was assigned to the deputy as a replacement. Thanks to the deputy's kindness and consideration, Boy could attend another refugee-school in Daejon while working as a houseboy.

The deputy was a retired British colonel and a veteran of both World War I and II. He had a Japanese bayonet scar on his leg and a bullet in his body. After he was discharged from the army following his injury, he served as a governor of a province of New Zealand. The deputy also loved Boy dearly. He enjoyed having Boy give a speech standing on a table in the American military officers' club. He would say to Boy, "When I return to England, you come with me. I'll send you to Oxford University, if you want."

While Boy was working as a houseboy, he met another houseboy who was well informed and a gifted speaker. Boy couldn't conceal his envy of his friend. He asked his friend's advice. Surprisingly, his friend's advice was unexpected. "I have a good idea for you. Why don't you go to church?"

"Church?"

"Yeah. All the church-goers are good at speaking, especially the revivalist preachers."

Boy hesitated before following his friend to a revival service. Whether due to his acute sensibilities at that early age or his impulsive temperament and tendency to fall head over heels in love with anybody and anything, Boy became a fanatical believer in Jesus the moment he entered a church. The revivalist speakers emphasized that for one's body to live, one has to breathe, eat and exercise; for one's soul to be alive, one has to pray, live on the words of the Bible, and evangelize. So Boy strove to practice, literally, what was preached. Almost every night he went to a revival meeting. He would pray all night long, fast, hand out leaflets of gospel on the streets and in school. During lunch hours, he would go up the hill behind the school, totally absorbed in praying, bible-reading and hymn-singing. In so doing, Boy missed out all the fun and frivolous pleasures of adolescence.

As it happened, one day, the retired British colonel collapsed, probably because of his chain-smoking and heavy drinking. He died of cancer six months before his scheduled return to England. Boy didn't cry, but once more Boy felt he had been abandoned.

Time passed and Boy became a young man.

Part Three

Chorus — Miracle of Inevitability

7 Watching the Night-Sea, Stars and Flowers

8 What Two Cherries Symbolize

9 Goldfish in a Bowl

10 I Accuse the Old Generation of Panderism

11 Cosmos in Dewdrops

12 Happy That I Loved Cosmos

Watching the Night-Sea, Stars and Flowers

"Love must not entreat or demand. Love must have the strength to become certain within itself. Then it ceases merely to be attracted and begins to attract . . . "

The moon rose in the night sea that was pouring with stars. The wind blowing along the shore carried with it a whiff of salt and fish. The man appeared on the shore. His shoulders drooping, he walked with a stagger. The floating moon and the adjoining stars lit the sky.

"Hi, Uncle." The child greeted Y as if he were expecting him.

"Why do you look the same?"

Avoiding the question, the child replied, "The night sea of the Earth is beautiful. That's because there are stars."

"That might be so."

The child seemed too preoccupied with his own thoughts to pay attention to what Y was saying. He carried on, saying reflectively, "Because the flowers are invisible to us, stars are beautiful."

Before Y could say anything, the child continued, "Uncle Y, have you met your cosmos?"

"I did, but she left me. I wonder if she sojourns in the night sea?"

Y was depressed and confused. He understood that one had to see things with the clear eye of a child who could not differentiate good from bad, clean from dirty, true from false and fearless from fearful. Only then could one share love that transcends the joys and sorrows of meeting and parting, the love that transcends the distance between time and space. And then one could realize the justification for the existence of everything in the world.

The same dewdrops sipped by a cicada become songs; sipped by a bee they become honey; whereas they become poison when imbibed by a snake. But we must not forget that even the venom of a snake can serve a purpose, Y reminded himself. The grown-up's greatest trouble is the loss of a child's eye.

Y was sick at heart, missing his Cosmos, and mused:

Though there's no telling whose providence it was for us, you and me, to meet and part, wouldn't it be like the blink of our eyes — like the twinkle of stars?

Though there's no telling why the snow and rainstorms come and go in and out of season, don't the dewdrops form at night on a blade of grass and vanish at sunrise as night melts into day like a mirage?

Though there's no telling what we're made of, aren't we all drops of life-giving and love-making that trickle into the sea of cosmos?

"Shall I share with you a story I once read?" Y asked.

"Fine. What's the story about?"

"It's about a young man who loved a star. The story is told in *Demian*, a visionary novel from an earthling by the name of Hermann Hesse," Y explained.

"That sounds quite interesting. I'd like to hear it," the child pleaded.

Frau Eva, Demian's mother, told her son's friend, Sinclair, about a youth who fell in love with a star. He stood by the sea, stretched out his arms and prayed to the star, dreamed of it and directed all his thoughts to it. But he knew, or felt he knew, that a star cannot be embraced by a human being. He considered it to be his fate to love a heavenly body without any hope of fulfillment. Out of this insight he constructed an entire philosophy of renunciation and silent, faithful suffering that would improve and purify him. Yet all his dreams reached the star. Once he stood on the high cliff, at night by the sea, and gazed at the star and burned with love for it. And at the height of his longing he leaped into the sky toward the star, but at the instant of leaping the thought of 'it's impossible' flashed through his mind. There he lay on the shore, shattered. He had not understood how to love. If at the instant of leaping he'd had the strength of faith in the fulfillment of his love, he would have soared into the heights and been united with the star.

Another time Frau Eva tells Sinclair a different story, concerning a lover whose love was unrequited. He withdrew completely within himself, believing his love would consume him. The world became lost to him. He no longer noticed blue sky and green woods; he no longer heard the brook murmur; his ears had turned deaf to the notes of the harp. Nothing mattered any more. He had become poor and wretched. Yet his love increased and he would rather have died, or been ruined, than renounce this beautiful woman. He felt his passion had consumed everything else within him and had become so strong, so magnetic that the beautiful woman must follow. She came to him and he stood with outstretched arms ready to draw her to him. As she stood before him, she was completely transformed, and with awe he felt and saw that he had won back all he had previously lost. She stood before him and surrendered herself to him. Sky, forest and brook all came toward him in new and resplendent colors, belonged to him, and spoke to him in his own language. And instead of merely winning the woman, he embraced the entire world, and every star in heaven glowed within him and sparkled with joy in his soul. He had loved and had found himself.

"Love must not entreat," she added, "or demand. Love must have the strength to become certain within itself. Then it ceases merely to be attracted and begins to attract. Sinclair, your love is attracted to me. Once it begins to attract me, I will come. I will not make a gift of myself, I must be won."

While Y was telling these stories, the child was falling fast asleep, and Y was going back to the days of his youth.

What Two Cherries Symbolize

Cosmos (C) seemed unaware of what she had done. The young man (Y) took the two cherries from C with a tremulous hand, as the symbol of the girl's virginity, and was thrilled.

When Y was serving in the Army, a fellow soldier received a weekly school paper sent by his girlfriend who attended The Ewha Women's University in Seoul. One day an article in the paper caught Y's fancy. The subject of the article was a letter shared by a professor and a student. The gist of what the professor wrote was that he used to send and receive 'romantic' letters in his younger days but nowadays his correspondence was all business. The professor added that no matter how brief it is, what you write reveals your soul.

The student's letter was the more challenging one. "We tend to lie more in correspondence than in conversation," she wrote. "Perhaps," she posited, "it was our common instinctive attempt to camouflage our shortcomings and human weaknesses; to embellish our achievements; to downplay our failures." And she ended by saying, "You'd think about the person who wrote or to whom you are writing — at least while reading or writing the letter."

Y judged her to be a modest, self-respecting person with a candid mind. "This is the very cosmo girl I've been looking for!" he decided.

He started writing his love letter addressed to her at school. To make sure his letters would be delivered promptly, they were sent by registered express mail. He not only sent letters but also his favorite Korean and foreign verses engraved on wood.

One was Yun Dong-Ju's 'Prologue' from *Sky, Wind, Stars and Poems* that was posthumously published. Yun Dong-Ju (1917-45) was the most celebrated Korean independence activist against the Japanese imperialist colonial rule of Korea. He died in a Japanese prison six months before World War II came to an end, as South African black activist Steve Biko (1946-77) died in police custody as a result of beatings received.

Yun Dong-Ju's 'Prologue'

Until the day I die, pray,
Not a speck to be ashamed of
Against the sky,
I suffered even for the leaves
Gently swaying in the breeze.

56

I've got to love all mortals
And I must walk along the path
Made for me.
Tonight, as always,
The stars are grazed
By the wind.

Another was a poem by William Blake (1757-1827):

To see a World in a Grain of Sand
And a Heaven in a Wild Flower.
Hold Infinity in the palm of your hand
And Eternity in an hour.

All were sent, together with records of Ludwig van Beethoven's symphonies, "Die Winter-reise," a song cycle of Franz Schubert, consisting of 24 songs set to poems of Wilhelm Muller, "The Magic Flute (Die Zauber-flote)," an opera by Wolfgang Amadeus Mozart, and a collection of Negro spirituals. Just in case C didn't have a record player, he even sent a portable one. Though he received no reply, he was confident she was getting her mail since there had been none marked "return to sender." So he kept on — untiringly.

After six months, Y got a reply to his daily one-way correspondence. C's home address was on the envelope. This was enough encouragement, and on a weekend pass to leave his military base,

Y was going to visit the girl he had been dreaming about night and day. His pulse fluttered and his stomach was full of butterflies.

The instant Y saw the girl in person, he could hardly breathe. The ecstasy of their first meeting was really beyond description. Her father, a celebrated poet, was kidnapped by the North during the Korean War. C was living with her novelist mother and a younger sister in a picture-perfect house in the suburbs.

C was excited, too. While receiving the mail from Y, she'd written a short story entitled *Man in Blue Uniform*, using Y as the major character, and she'd just been notified by post that her story was a winner in a literary contest.

"When I receive the prize money, I'll send you a gift subscription to Sassanggye, *World of Thoughts*," then a popular highbrow monthly magazine, which was later forced to cease publication by the military government.

A few days after the C's notice of winning, Y went to the award ceremony to congratulate C on making her debut as a writer, carrying a gift set of fountain pens. For some reason, C didn't show and Y picked up the prize on her behalf and took it to her home. C was away, and Y left the gift of pens with her mother.

When Y left C's home to return to his base after visiting her for the third time, it began to rain. Before they left for the bus stop, C picked two cherries from her garden and handed them to Y. C seemed unaware of what she had done. Holding the two cherries in his hand, Y thrilled at the symbolism. The early summer rain soaked through the tear in the umbrella, quickening their pulses and warming their breaths. Seeing Y off at the bus stop, C agreed to another date the following weekend.

Goldfish in a Bowl

Y didn't feel sad or pain, lying in a military hospital bed after taking a beating from a mob of KATUSA (Korean Augmentation to the U.S. Army stationed in Korea), for he had in his heart of hearts two cherries from C, so sweet and precious.

When Y took the last bus to his base the night of their third date, all the passengers were members of KATUSA except one lone GI. Many were clearly drunk.

"That Yankee is all by himself, isn't he? I feel lousy. Shall we beat him up?"

"Oh yeah, why not?"

"Yeah, yeah, all Yanks are SOBs. Why don't we tell them to leave us alone and just go back to their own country?"

They were calling the quietly-sitting GI names in Korean, even though they could speak English.

"Let's stop this, for goodness' sake. It's such a cowardly attack on a helpless guy!" Y protested.

Though hearing these admonishing words, the noisy crowd failed to quiet down.

"What? Cowardly? Don't you dare say that again."

Following a momentary silence, someone spat.

"Aren't we all members of KATUSA defending our country with the help of the U.S. Army?" Y gently reminded his fellow soldier passengers.

Then someone else yelled, "Hey, driver, stop the bus!"

When the driver pulled over, a mob of KATUSA members dragged Y out of the bus and bombarded him with kicks and punches. When he opened his eyes he was in a military hospital, enveloped in bandages.

His face was swollen from the beatings, yet he didn't feel himself aggrieved. Instead he commiserated with the attackers. He was aware, only too well, how they were being treated by their American comrades-in-arms. They were constantly subject to ridicule and humiliation. So he understood that he was an easy prey for them to vent their pent-up rage and frustration.

In February 1961, Y enlisted with the Republic of Korean Army. On completing a basic and adjunctive training, he was posted to the Aviation Wing of the Capital Division. Because of his spinal surgery, he had to wear a corset and was excused from strenuous physical exercises.

Allowed just to sit and watch, he was nicknamed 'The Head Monk of Hae-In-Sa,' a well-known Buddhist temple in Korea.

Stationed at a military airstrip that was busy with helicopters and reconnaissance planes taking off and landing, Y served as an interpreter for Korean and American pilots and other officers. One day he caught the attention of the commanding general of the 8th U.S. Army and was transferred to KATUSA. He was assigned to the U.S. Army Chemical Depot and the U.S. Army 547 Engineer Corps stationed in Buchon County, Kyungkee Province, near Kimpo Airport. There were hundreds of KATUSA members and scores of Korean civilian employees, besides U.S. Army personnel, at the base.

Under the chain of command headed by a ROK Army officer, a major, and followed by officers of junior rank, sergeants 1st class, staff sergeants and sergeants, KATUSA members were doing all sorts of menial tasks — from cleaning mess halls and utensils, grass-cutting, snow-shoveling, loading and unloading, to repairing roads — almost like slaves. They were often insulted as 'slicky boys,' meaning petty thieves, by the GIs. Even so, the ROK Army soldiers were eager to become KATUSA members for the comfort and con-venience of better facilities and provisions at the U.S. Army bases.

Y, too, was incensed by the insulting remarks. They enraged him by their deliberate and continual injustice. But he couldn't blame the Americans. Koreans were, in part, responsible for the ill treatment, he thought.

Y decided to write an open letter to his fellow KATUSA mem-bers, reminding them that one has to behave like a decent human being in order to be treated like one: "Let's become excellent emis-saries representing Korean people."

Y instantly became a trouble-maker to those in charge of KA-TUSA personnel. Those in charge were, in fact, responsible for all the corrupt and shameless practices going on that brought all the disgrace and dishonor to all the Korean people and KATUSA members.

He received several threatening warnings. One was, "If you want to save your life, go back to the ROK Army."

Becoming a fugitive was out of question.

One evening, a gang of former street bullies and martial arts experts dragged him to a little valley some distance away. He did not forget an old saying, "If you don't lose your head and heart, you can survive a tiger's attack."

Y was always more spirited whenever he was challenged. Years before, it was a sports day at his grade school. He was the runner in the last leg of a relay race. One foot was badly cut by a broken piece of glass during a soccer match earlier in the day and had been wrapped, yet he ran faster than usual to victory with a long trail of bandage soaked in blood, prompting a thunderous applause.

Even though Y exercised on parallel and high bars in grade school, practiced judo in middle/high school and Taekwondo in college, he was no match for the villains armed with baseball bats, metal bars and knives. He used to engage black-belt-holders and was, more often than not, victorious, but obstinately refused to be graded and wear belts in any color. It was his credo to go against the grain, believing "no technique is the best technique."

Surrounded by more than ten guys that night in the valley, still, he could see each of them as a big softie, or a timorous soul — not a real tough guy. He'd been observing closely that in movies, as well as in real-life events, the outcome was decided well before the fight even began, be it an argument, a fist fight, a sword fight or a gun fight. Whoever cowers first becomes the vanquished.

Y, though smaller in size, must have had more guts to over-power his opponents. After disengaging himself from those poor guys thrown into disarray, frightened out of their senses, he returned to the base and held a ballot of KATUSA members. If the majority cast a vote of 'no confidence' in him, he proposed to return to the ROK Army. The vote was unanimous with a few abstentions, pleading him not to go and urging him on as he cleaned up the mess. Only the officers in charge left, as the official order for the return of all the non-commissioned officers was revoked at the last minute — at Y's request. In those days, KATUSA members dreaded being sent back to the ROK Army. In their place, he was given overall responsibility for KATUSA personnel as a Non-Commissioned Officer In Charge with a double promotion of rank from private first class to sergeant.

After improving the moral fiber of KATUSA personnel, Y had to fight hard for equal rights. In an effort to reason with the over-bearing GIs, he wrote another open letter, this time in English, to all the U.S. military officers and enlisted men stationed in Korea. He called their attention to the fact that no matter how deeply grateful Korean people in the South were to the U.S. Forces fighting against Communist North Korea, the American military had come to Korea, first and foremost, for the interest of the U.S.A. They wanted to keep South Korea as its advance stronghold between the U.S. and the Soviet Union. "Was it just to play a Savior or Santa Claus for charity?" he asked in earnest. Wasn't it much less to colonize Korea in the name of Democracy and Capitalism; still less to incite anti-Americanism by fault-finding and trampling on the human rights and pride of Korean people? He wrote, citing a passage or two like: "A great man shows his greatness by the way he treats a little man." and "The manner of giving shows the character of the giver more than the gift itself."

"Let's remember Jesus' words that man lives not by bread alone," he suggested.

Y was fearful that his letter might have repercussions for the whole KATUSA contingent serving with the U.S. Army. The effect of the letter, however, was unexpectedly beneficial to all concerned. Y won the official commendation with 'a letter of appreciation' from the commanding officer of the U.S. Army detachment for raising the morale of KATUSA personnel and making a very positive contribution to the successful close cooperation with the U.S. Forces.

Y was happy. Even though he had been hospitalized following the beating by fellow KATUSA members, because of the two cherries he received from C that night, he was euphoric. What does it matter if he lost a few pennies, now that he owned the most precious treasure of treasures?

I Accuse the Old Generation of Panderism

Yet again, maybe it wasn't meant to be. 'Ah! Was it you? Though stars are shining in the sky. . . No matter how hard I try, my efforts are in vain…I couldn't hold your cold hand and warm it up. . . ' like operatic aria lyrics.

Twilight was approaching. It was a piece of thin blue spreading across the crumpled drawing paper of Y's sketchbook.

Y received a 'Dear John' letter from C. It came out of the blue. It happened the very next day after he told of his major at college and of his younger brother who didn't go to college. What do you learn in college, Y had to ask himself. If all that a college education fosters is arrogance and vanity, then he would take it as a consolation that his brother didn't go to such a factory that mass-produces 'human parasites.' He wouldn't recommend a higher education to anybody and he wouldn't marry a college graduate — he swore.

Her mother's viewpoint was easy to understand. Among all the available suitors, why not some with more practical value, such as medicine, law or economics? Had he gone to a Divinity School, at least he could have become a church minister or a priest. He wouldn't be able to feed her daughter. She must have been dismayed.

"What school did you go to?" She asked Y when he'd made his first visit.

"I went to the College of Liberal Arts and Sciences, Seoul National University, the most prestigious university in Korea." With that, she might have expected that he had attended the department of Political Science or English. Asked about his siblings, he told her that a sister was studying abroad. So the assumption that he was from a well-to-do family turned out to be incorrect in the light of the fact that his younger brother never went to college. It was hard for a parent to grasp and accommodate the discrepancy. He understood the reason for the abrupt break-up. It had to do with a child's future security.

Until then, Y always withdrew at once whenever his advances to a girl were not welcome — even if not rejected outright. But this time, it didn't seem C's rejection was due to her own volition at all. He kept on pleading with her by telephone and in writing not to follow anybody's dictates but to follow her own heart and soul. His entreaty was of no avail. He even sought her younger sister's moral support. If one could move heaven and earth, why not another human being? But the two sisters seemed unable to free themselves from their mother's absolute influence on them. Y became desperate and wrote a poem entitled "I Accuse the Old

Generation of Panderism." He addressed it to C's mother and her two daughters and mailed it.

On the day he was discharged from the armed forces, Y hurried to C's home. As he rang the doorbell, C peeped over the wall and bolted the gate securely before disappearing into the house. He jumped over the wall, as if to rescue the princess imprisoned in a castle — like Hong Kil-Dong, Korea's most legendary outlaw. He then knocked on the door. Meanwhile, she ran barefoot to fetch her aunt — a neighbor, he discovered later.

What baffled and even angered Y was the fact that C's mother was a famous writer of distinction, who was supposed to lead the way in love as well as in life. How could such a mentor so cruelly nip young love?

Y grimly held out hope. From somewhere a thin piece of aurora began spreading across the crumpled drawing paper of his romantic sketchbook.

Cosmos in Dewdrops

One day Y chanced upon C and began following her. She was already a young lady, no longer a girlish figure.

It was one of those days when Y was wandering aimlessly around the streets like a sleepwalker half awake from a sweet dream. She entered the building of *The Korea Herald*, an English-language daily published in Seoul. He learned from the front desk guard that she was working in the paper's research department.

Out of military service, Y went back to school, attending The Hankuk University of Foreign Studies in Seoul while running a bookstore, The Dukhae Book Gallery. The name was a combination of the first letter/character of his mother's first name, Duk-soon, and that of his pen name, Haesim, with Dukhae — 덕해 in Korean alphabet and 德海 in Chinese characters — meaning 'The Sea of Virtue.'

One morning Y happened to read an article in *The Korea Times*, another English-language daily published in Seoul. It was written by an American wife of a Korean man. She wrote about human relationships, especially between a man and a woman. The article provoked discussion. He wrote to the editor, presenting his own thoughts, which were based on his pen pal experience. Much to his surprise, his article appeared in the same column the next day. He took a copy to show to C. If it wasn't her own idea to sever their relationship so suddenly, would she reconsider her decision and resume seeing him?

"I'll think about it and let you know shortly," she replied.

Y didn't hear from C for some time.

Meanwhile, there was an oratorical contest in English for students sponsored by *The Korea Herald*. "I accuse the old generation of panderism," Y roared. By sheer coincidence, *The Korea Herald* was currently advertising for new reporters. Y finished top in the written exam and interview and became a reporter.

A few days later, someone wanted to see him. It was a former reporter of *The Korea Herald* who had recently left, joining a new Korean-language daily *The Joongang Ilbo*.

"I understand that you and Miss C had a brief acquaintanceship in the past. I've been dating Miss C for several months and we are going to get married soon. So give her up, if you please," the reporter formally requested.

Y felt challenged, "If Miss C were a slave or mere chattel, perhaps we could fight a duel to take her," he replied. "But it's up to her, isn't it?"

"If you want to hear what she has to say, I'll arrange a meeting, if I may," the guy said.

"You don't need to do that. I'll find out myself," Y responded with a smirk. He went straight to C.

"Didn't you accuse the old generation of panderism?" She asked. "Since you called my mom a 'madam,' you treated me like a prostitute. How could I see a man again who insulted us so cruelly?" Her answer was an unequivocal no.

"I understand. I won't bother you any more," Y replied. "Please accept my sincere apologies. I'll wish you all the happiness." And then he added, "I just want you to remember that though a dewdrop vanishes without a trace when it evaporates, it was a dewdrop real and true while it was a dewdrop."

"What do you mean by that?" C protested.

Y gave a wry smile and left.

When he returned home, Y recited from Kahlil Gibran's *The Garden of the Prophet*, a lyrical celebration of the mystical beauty of Nature:

The image of the morning sun in a dewdrop is not less than the sun. The reflection of life in your soul is not less than life.

The dewdrop mirrors the light because it is one with light, and you reflect life because you and life are one.

When darkness is upon you, say: 'This darkness is dawn not yet born; and though night's travail be full upon me, yet shall dawn be born unto me even as unto the hills.'

The dewdrop rounding its sphere in the dusk of the lily is not unlike yourself gathering your soul in the heart of God.

Shall a dewdrop say: 'But once in a thousand years am I even a dewdrop,' speak you and answer it saying: 'Know you not that the light of all the years is shining in your circle?'

And Y mused:

> Was the grass wet with early morning dew
> to pay your dues of life and love?
> Were they dewdrops of life-giving and love-making,
> or rather teardrops of joy and sorrow?
> Was that for breathing in this magic world to the full,
> and breathing out to the last, before transforming back
> into the mystical essence of the cosmos?

Y then handed in his resignation and joined *The Korea Times* and opened a pub for moonlighting. He named the pub Haesim, 해심 (in Korean), and '海心' (in Chinese), meaning 'The Heart of The Sea,' the pen name he gave himself in childhood. It became very popular with romantics — the students of life and love.

Happy That I Loved Cosmos

The days passed and Y became a man. As it happened, twenty-five years later C and Y met again — this time in New York in 1988. They were finally united. Yet again, it was brief. Must it be in the bud, as the saying in Latin goes: "Finis Origine Pendet." (The beginning foretells the end.)

Was it a happenstance that *Love in the Time of Cholera*, a love story by Gabriel Garcia Marques, was published in the same year? The novel begins with this opening sentence: "IT WAS IN-EVITABLE."

In their youth, Florentino and Fermina fall passionately in love. When Fermina eventually chooses to marry a wealthy doctor, Florentino is devastated. At first nothing seems inevitable, only an unreciprocated love affair. But his prayers are answered after some fifty years. Was this a true story? Was what happened to Y and C inevitable?

Y recalled what Frau Eva in Hermann Hesse's *Demian* said:

73

"You must not give way to desires which you don't believe in. . . . You should, however, either be capable of renouncing these desires or feel wholly justified in having them. Once you are able to make your request in such a way that you will be quite certain of its fulfillment, then the fulfillment will come."

They met again.

C and her younger sister became famous novelists themselves — like their mother. Each of the two sisters was the recipient of a prestigious literary prize in Korea. While they were together for ten months, C wrote a two-volume novel titled *Man with Flowers*, sort of a sequel to *Man in Blue Uniform*, a short story she composed as her debut piece to win a prize a quarter of a century earlier. For both works she used Y as the main character.

To be sad, or satisfied, with the truth that you get to keep your child in your arms only until the child leaves the nest may be a choice, not a temperament. He wished her all the happiness once more, for the last time, as she flew away into 'the sky of arts' after taking as much nourishment as she needed from 'the nest of life' he provided.

Y was happy that he loved C.

Part Four— Solo Again
May My Heart be the Sea of Cosmos!

13 Cosmic Sound of Child-Song

14 A Collapsed Bachelor-Tower

15 Unexpected Opportunity

16 Everything is a Miracle

17 Postnatal Education — Name

18 Our Self-Portrait — Froglike

Cosmic Sound of Child-Song

Always changing and impermanent though life is,

Troubled and sorrowful though life is,

Isn't it so much better to be born than not to be born at all?

Isn't it felicity in life to love somebody,

Even if you may be crossed in love and heartbroken?

The years passed and Y became an old man. He and the child were resting on the shore, looking up at the sky strewn with stardust.

Gazing at the stars, the child said, "Why don't you ask me where I come from?"

Y responded, "Even when you go back, you'll still be in my heart. So it really doesn't matter whether you leave or stay."

"That's true. Do you still miss your Cosmos?"

"Of course, everything is the sea of cosmos for me."

After a bit of silence, Y continued, "I've grown old now. I'm at the age to compose a poem eulogizing my own death beforehand."

"What's that?" the child asked with a grimace.

"In actual fact, it's a eulogy to life."

The child became very quiet.

Y shed tears, thinking aloud, "How much more precious is a moment of human existence than the eternity of divinity meaningless to mortals?"

Raising his body, Y looked at the night sea. There was the sea of cosmos spread out in front of him. Y paused for a moment, then went on to elaborate on the 'eulogy to life,' "Greek philosopher Epicurus' dictum 'carpe diem' epitomizes his philosophy of life. This two-word phrase literally means 'to seize the day.' It is used to urge someone to make the most of the present time and give little thought to the future; to enjoy the present, as opposed to placing all the hope in the future. It also presents youth as ephemeral and advises the pursuit of pleasure.

"The truth is," Y continued, "children are the embodiment of happiness, enjoying life instinctively as the great practitioners of this maxim of Epicurean philosophy. Even their cries are not cries but shrieks of laughter; the cosmic sound of child-song; the ancient music of joy and thankfulness. They are our native symphonic tunes in rhythm with the sea to celebrate our original blessing and our ultimate destination. It's our cosmic chorus: 'star one, me one; star two, me two; star three, me three. . . ' This is the Cosmos Cantata."

The child remained silent. There was only the celestial music of all the stars in the wind blowing from the sea. Sitting next to the child, Y saw the stars of the night-sea and had a vision of cosmos flowering everywhere. Looking back on his earlier days, he was amazed at what had happened all along. Y took a walk down memory lane.

A Collapsed Bachelor-Tower

Y never married C. A bastion of Y's virginity collapsed unexpectedly. Repulsed by grownups' self-righteous hypocrisy from early on, Y posed as 'a lamb in wolf's clothing.' His crude behavior attracted many girls, but despite his vulgar language, he had always acted like a saint — until one fateful night.

As if a monkey falls from a tree by an unforeseen accident under the influence of alcohol, Y happened to sleep with a girl without having had a date with her.

Feeling morally responsible, Y proposed to marry her. But this very smart and independent-minded young woman, to his great surprise, rejected him, saying they didn't have to get married just because they'd had sex.

Having always believed that 'action speaks louder than words,' Y decided to go by her action, not by her words, and tried hard to persuade her to marry him. To make the matter worse, her family put up strong opposition.

Undeterred, and more determined to overcome all adversities,

Y persevered and, two years later, they married, but the marriage ended two years after that. Soon after getting a divorce, he learned that she was pregnant with their third child. So he decided to re-marry her and to make their marriage work for the sake of the children.

After trying harder for eighteen more years, however, they were divorced for the second time due to their intrinsic and un-remitting incompatibility. Y learned, the hard way, that you can't change yourself, let alone others. A cat is a cat. It cannot become a dog or vice versa — so to speak.

Perhaps it was a wrong match from the beginning. Had they truly loved each other, they might have been able to transcend all the differences, difficulties, shortcomings and misfortunes.

In retrospect, since early childhood, Y had been influenced by sayings of great people. Brainwashed and hypnotized, he would tell himself that his was a big fire, unlike a candle's flame or a small fire easily extinguished even by a breeze. No, his was more like an eternal star that comes to shine as soon as the sky is dark enough or like a kite that rises highest against the wind — not with it. Thus he was never discouraged by anything. On the contrary, he was ever more heartened and inspired, come what may!

Striving desperately for almost four scores, Y came to realize, at last, that nothing can be forced. Anything that's meant to happen will happen, and if it is not meant to happen, it never will — no matter what.

Unexpected Opportunity

One never knows what's in store. What seemed impossible, like catching a heavenly star, could sometimes happen in real life. Whenever Y went to Kimpo Airport near Seoul to welcome or see someone off, those privileged to walk up or down a boarding ramp were aliens from other planets to him.

At one time Y was saddened by the news that hundreds of people lost their lives in an airplane crash over the East Sea between Korea and Japan. At the same time he was even more shocked by a disturbing thought crossing his mind. It was Schadenfreude, a feeling of pleasure at the bad things that happen to other people. For a moment he couldn't help feeling the joy of seeing the fall of the 'high-flyers,' the envy of the 'low-crawlers' and he could commiserate with the country boys throwing rocks at passing trains.

An unexpected opportunity came his way. After working for an American educational publisher as their Korean representative for two years, Y was offered a transfer to Australia. But in those days, the Australian government didn't issue a permanent resident visa to a non-European. He was sent to the United Kingdom, instead.

It took a whole month for his family, with three young children — aged three months to three years — to make the journey overseas to London from Seoul. Making the most of this unimaginable chance to travel abroad with his family, Y had stopovers for sightseeing in Tokyo, Hong Kong, Bangkok, Rome, Athens, Paris and Amsterdam.

Upon arrival in England, Y found the civil, but cool, reception, a mixture of condescension and reserve hard to take. The English 'gentlemen' he had to work with seemed to have a hangover from their memories and sentiments of bygone Pax Britannica days.

Y was subject to all kinds of subtle, implicit discrimination. He could understand why they must have felt affronted. Why on earth did they have to bring someone from an almost unheard of backward place called Korea — as if there were no competent people in the U.K.?

Determined not to become a laughing stock and sent back, Y worked like mad. He traveled throughout Great Britain, including Wales and Scotland, to visit all the universities and colleges. He presented new titles for textbook adoptions and library orders. He represented about 50 American publishers whose publications were distributed all over the world by his employer — an international corporation. Besides holding more than 200 book exhibitions a year, he attended academic conferences for market research. In so doing, he compiled an up-to-date mailing list of faculty members and librarians and contributed to a large increase in sales.

He was away from home and with his family briefly on weekends. Even so, he was satisfied with results that made it all worthwhile.

Everything is a Miracle

The old cliché, "Where there's a will, there's a way" still rings true to a firm believer in the truism. In a legal battle carried on with the daring of a hopeless and helpless desperado to break a rock with an egg, Y won in the end by a unanimous decision.

While Y was settling in doing 'a great job,' he was offered another transfer, this time to Singapore. But the terms were unacceptable. Relocation costs provided made no allowance for his housing and children's education. Singaporean nationals lived in their government-subsidized, low-cost apartments and their children went to Chinese-speaking local public schools free of charge. Y couldn't afford to send his children to an English-speaking international school. The private school fee for one child was more than his annual salary. When he declined the offer of transfer, he was made redundant in his job. Severance pay was only a week's wage for each year he worked in the U.K. They wouldn't pay the moving expenses and airplane tickets for his family to return to Korea. They were not obligated because it was not stipulated in the contract. It was an oversight on his part not to have asked for a revised written contract of employment when he was being transferred from Korea.

Unable to return to Korea, or to seek a new employment, prohibited by the work permit his former employer had obtained for Y to work in the U.K., his family of five was stranded in a foreign land.

Y consulted with half a dozen lawyers in London. They told him he had no case legally, though morally he did. In their opinion, his former employer was not at fault. They paid him severance pay in accordance with legal requirements.

Surprisingly, a couple of national papers and a local daily reported on the plight of his family — but to no avail. A Labor Party Member of Parliament representing the district where his family resided wrote a formal letter on his behalf, threatening to raise the issue in the British Parliament. He had a meeting with an executive of Y's former employer. Still, all the efforts were in vain.

As a last resort, Y went to the Industrial Tribunal. His former employer was represented by a group of American and British lawyers. Since Y had no money to hire a lawyer, and no lawyer offered to represent him, he had to represent himself.

At the end of a year-long trial came a judgment from the Tribunal. The chairman and his two supporting judges heard the case. It was a unanimous decision that Y was unfairly dismissed.

Everybody complimented and congratulated him on his victory, even the company's lawyers. The British media reported on his case as a story of "Boy David beating Goliath."

A sure thing in the world. There's all the beauty one cares to behold; all the magic and mystery to wonder, as a child marvels, that stars can exist. From one's birth onward, each breath taken in and out, each moment to live and love, everything is a miracle, be it a blade of grass, a flower, a dewdrop, a raindrop, a snowflake, a ray of moonlight or sunlight, the twinkle of stars, the wind, the sea, the sky, the cosmos. All are more than miracles, infinitely mysterious and sorrowfully and sadly beautiful.

Postnatal Education — Name

Like Hae-a, everybody living on earth must be protected by one's own guardian angel. Otherwise, how could anyone live through rough times — all the disasters, calamities, and catastrophes? One never knows what to expect from one day to the next, as the landscape, seascape, moonscape and dreamscape are always changing.

If 'head-works' were thoughts, 'heart-works' might be called arts. From early childhood, Y liked songs and enjoyed music, being sentimental and sensitive to everything like all children. When he heard a song, the words fascinated him and he was instantly carried away by the melodies.

But was Y born tone-deaf? He couldn't sing along with the music. Then what made his three children major in music?

The first thing Y did in his married life was to buy a piano, a deluxe stereo system and hundreds of records in an effort to make it up to his wife. Her family almost disowned her for marrying Y with no prospects or fortune to inherit. She left her piano at her parents' home, a gift on her entering a prestigious girls' middle school in Seoul. The stereo system and many records she bought with her own money, earned as a bank employee after college, were also left behind with her parents. Since she didn't continue to play the piano regularly, it was less functional and more decorative. But after her children were born, the piano became a toy again which she could play with them. To Y, who grew up like a street urchin, the Western classical music was something a child born with a silver spoon in one's mouth could indulge in, just like the upstarts who monopolized playing golf in South Korea after the 'Liberation' of Korea from the Japanese at the end of World War II.

When Y's family moved to England, his children went to a local school in Luton, Bedfordshire. One day, an itinerant music teacher visited the school his oldest child, Hae-a, attended. Pupils interested in learning to play an instrument were given just a ten-minute lesson a week and instruments were loaned to them by the school. Thus began music lessons for his children, one after another, the oldest and the youngest on the violin and the middle one on the cello. Before long, a few months after they started making all kinds of noise, they had to leave England for Hawaii where their grandma and two aunts lived. Short though it was, they must have enjoyed the lessons enough to practice hard and do well. Their music teachers were sad that they had to leave.

Soon after they arrived in Hawaii, Y received a letter inviting them to return. He was deeply grateful to the music teachers who made arrangements for an audition at the Chetham's School of Music in Manchester, England. No matter how slim a chance it was, he couldn't throw it away. He would rather cast away all the money for the airfares. Although he didn't expect any of his girls to pass the audition, he was not going to deprive them of a thousandth of a one percent chance of success. Much to everyone's surprise, all three passed and were accepted. But it was a very expensive boarding school — way beyond his means. So there was nothing they could do about it. They were just about to go back to Hawaii when the school offered full scholarships to the three little sisters, a godsend undreamed of.

Thus it came to pass that the children left home early, at the ages of seven to ten. Had music been forced upon them, they would have feigned interest at first but they would have quit too soon. This seemed to be an example of the effect of one's own inclination. If one liked it, whatever it was, one couldn't help doing it with enthusiasm without even making an effort — and it became so much fun.

In the hope that his children would stay young and childlike forever; that they would love everything and not miss a thing, Y named them with one common syllable "a" '아' in Korean alphabet, (meaning 'child' in Chinese character '兒') in their first names. Praying they would live on the cosmic energy of the sea, the sky and the stars, he named them with another Chinese character in each name as Hae-a, 해아, 海兒, meaning the Sea-child; Su-a, 수아, 秀兒, meaning the Sky-child (of excellence); Song-a, 성아, 星兒, meaning

90

the Star-child. Didn't the American Native Indians go into the woods for a revelation as to what to name themselves? Long may they continue to live up to their names like a long-lasting couple growing to look alike in time.

All children are very dear to their parents. But sometimes, some children make all-too-serious grown-ups laugh their heads off or scare them to death.

Y's youngest daughter, Song-a, displayed her star quality from early days. Thank her lucky star for its namesake! She did her impressions of celebrities on T.V. and everybody was captivated by her performance. Even before she went to a nursery school, she would shoo away all the boys flocking around her like a swarm of flies. She would do so without uttering a sound. She just gave them a sharp look or the lyric expression on the face. She would talk down to grown-ups, using more grown-up vocabulary. Y couldn't admonish her. Every time he tried to do so, he was instantly disarmed. When he yelled at her in a burst of anger, she put him in his place right off by raising her tiny index finger to her pretty lips or whispering in his ear, "You don't have to shout." And he hushed.

At times she seemed to be a dainty sprite popped out of a myth or a fairy tale. When he appeared to be lecturing her about her homework, she looked him straight in the eye like a child looking at a gorilla behind the bars in a zoo. When he went to the bathroom, she was there right behind him and surprised him peeing. And she asked, "Dad, did you shake?"

Y's middle one, Su-a, was extraordinary — even as an infant. Was that due to her name? Was she a born rebel? She wouldn't do anything if she were told to do it. If she were told not to do it, she would do it one way or another. Whatever she did, she did as much and when she wanted. That's why people called her "Crazy Super Su-a." Once her interest was awakened, there was no stopping her. When she laughed, she would roll over and over on the floor. Life was a time for play and the world was her playground. This little playgirl never stopped until she had exhausted herself. No wonder she would often fall asleep at the dinner table. She was a fearless adventurer.

After Y's family arrived in England on February 14, 1972, they lived in a rented house in Kings Langley, Hertfordshire. One Sunday morning he looked into the children's bedroom. The oldest and the youngest were still asleep. But the middle one's bed was empty. He found her downstairs. She was in a complete daze after taking a whole bottle of baby-aspirins as if they were candies. Apparently one-and-a-half-year-old Su-a climbed up a high chair at the breakfast table and took the bottle out of a medicine cabinet in the kitchen. She was rushed to the hospital and her life was saved. That summer they were vacationing in Cornwall in S.W. England. They rented a camper on a hill near the beach. While preparing the breakfast one morning, he looked out the window and saw their car, parked next to the camper, was slowly moving down the hill. Even more shocking was a live daredevil stunt action of two-year-old Su-a jumping out of the driver's seat from the rolling car. What if she had been run over by the car? The car crashed into a ditch at the bottom of the hill. She must have climbed into the car and released the handbrake.

At one time when Su-a was three, Y came home at the weekend as usual from his weekly business trip. He had a lot to tell his wife. But Su-a kept interrupting them and she got a scolding from her mother for not waiting until they finished talking. Still, she didn't stop and tried desperately to engage him in conversation. Beginning to get annoyed with her persistence, he yelled at her to shut up. She didn't even blink. "Dad, now *you* talk to Mom," she replied, with a nonchalant shrug and left the room. Su-a always had to have the last word in any argument. She was so quick-witted, most often one or two steps ahead of everybody. When they went shopping, not sure what to buy, they usually asked Su-a for a smart choice. Talking to Su-a, Y burst out laughing time and again, waving an invisible flag of unconditional surrender, for she had already presented a more convincing counter-argument even before he could make out a case.

Soon after her older sister, Hae-a, started on the violin, unbeknownst to her parents Su-a went to Hae-a's violin teacher to ask for a cello teacher, saying she liked the cello sound better. The day she came home with a quarter-size cello loaned by her school, she kept scraping away at the cello for six hours, skipping supper altogether.

Later, after taking a couple of lessons, Su-a followed Hae-a to a rehearsal for the Youth Orchestra concert in the evening. The rest of them arrived at the concert hall in good time. Until the concert started Su-a didn't come to sit with them. Y was beginning to feel nervous and distinctly uneasy about Su-a's whereabouts. The moment he looked at the stage, he was frightened out of his wits and almost fainted. Seven-year-old Su-a was playing in the orchestra, sitting on the edge of a chair with her legs dangling over the sides of her tiny cello among much bigger children — including high school students.

Y thought it must be on account of her name. He thought, too, long may it continue.

Y's firstborn Hae-a, her quiet and calm outward appearance notwithstanding, was a child of 'inexhaustible' energy and passion, brimming with confidence and courage, her teachers used to remark in her school report cards.

Was perception reality? As Hae-a came into being, it was the realization of what Y wished, imagined and dreamed. While his wife was expecting twins, he named them Hae-a, 해아, in Korean alphabet meaning 'the child of the sun' and Hae-a, 海兒 in Chinese characters meaning 'the child of the sea,' as his personal mantra for them to be 'sunny' and 'romantic.' But then they were born premature and put in incubators. One survived and the other one became the surviving twin's guardian angel.

May Hae-a, Su-a, Song-a and everybody else sojourning on earth have no bad weather, only different kinds of good weather, rain or shine!

Y traveled light right back to the future. Many moons ago, when he was working as a houseboy, his two surrogate father figures, one American and the other one British, promised to send him to The Juilliard School and to Oxford University, but it was not to be. Even so, his two children went there instead, Hae-a to Oxford and Su-a to The Juilliard.

Our Self-Portrait — Froglike

One day, while clearing a blocked gutter under the edge of the roof of his house in a suburb of London, Y found something strange growing there. He couldn't tell if they were plants or mineral deposits. They were hard, in the shape of tiny stars, strange objects of curiosity, wonder and mystery. He gave some of them to his children so that they could show them to their teachers and friends. Whatever their substance might be, he thought, they must have come to bear an uncanny resemblance to the stars they were singing and whispering through, night and day. It recalled a fairy tale of a hunchback Persian princess who became straight by stretching herself daily in front of her straight-backed statue. He had a sudden awakening to the natural phenomena common everywhere, in the air, on land and beneath the ocean, with sunflowers and starfish serving as constant reminders.

A summer day, years ago, Y's family vacationed in the Caribbean. Early one morning he went out for a walk on the shore. It just so happened that he spotted a tropical fish jumping up and down, unable to return to the water after the ebb tide. He quickly scooped the fish up in his two hands formed into a bowl and let it go back to the sea. The next morning he found a beautiful conch shell at the same spot where he'd rescued the fish. To him, the conch shell seemed to be a 'thank-you gift' from the fish.

As someone once said, to be certain about anything in life was the privilege of a fool because there was only one thing to be certain of — that there was nothing to be certain of.

What decided how you started in life and how you developed? Was it happenstance or heavenly providence? Be that as it may, there is no denying that you are a product of birth and circumstance. If you were eagle-born, how could you laugh at a snail for being so low and slow? It might be possible that the snail dying to be an eagle became a frog after trying so hard for so long, just as animals wishing to be godlike developed into humans.

Y couldn't recall whether he saw this lyrically ungrammatical portrait — drawn by somebody — of humans from the swamplands in a dream or in his waking hours:

What a wonderful bird
The frog are!
When he stand, he sits
Almost,
When he hops he flys almost.
He ain't got no sense hardly,
He ain't got no tail hardly,

Either.
When he sit, he sit on what
He ain't got, almost.

Y felt his own soliloquy was voiced by a kindred spirit by the
name of William Wordsworth, the celebrated English poet laureate,
one hundred and sixty-odd years earlier in his famous poem:

My heart leaps up,
When I behold
A Rainbow in the sky;
So was it when I was a Child
So is it now I am a Man
So be it when I shall grow old,
Or let me die!
The Child is Father of the Man;
And I could wish my days to be
Bound each to each
By natural piety.

Afterword: All's Wondrous Serendipity

Let's imagine we live forever. Let's imagine we are young forever. Then that wouldn't be living or being young. Then we wouldn't be able to appreciate life, to love life.

Walt Whitman sings in his "Song of Myself": "To die is different from what anyone supposed, and luckier." In *Leaves of Grass* he wrote: "I sing the body electric," — as a scintillating metaphor — "My flesh and blood playing out lightning to strike what is hardly different from myself." Scottish writer Sir James Matthew Barrie presents the foresight in his internationally and abidingly famous children's play, *Peter Pan*: "To die will be an awfully big adventure." No wonder the Sufis say, "Life is a dream, and death is waking up."

There's an old Greek saying that life is a tragedy to a feeling person and a comedy to a thinking person. Shouldn't we say that life is, above all, an adventure and that love is the adventure of adventures?

In retrospect, all the truly wonderful things in my life always happened to me in the most unexpected moments. Things I was quite sure that would happen never did, and what did, usually happened much later than I wished. So I learned by experience that the best way not to be disappointed and preferring instead to be happily surprised is to be prepared right from the outset for the very worst, rather than hoping for the best. Am I then a pessimist, not an optimist? I think I'm neither. Early on I decided to be a "contentist," contenting myself with doing my best and utmost and with being my true self, the way I was born to be, be the outcome what it may.

Precociously realizing that almost everything from birth onwards was beyond my choice and control, I learned to be happy and thankful for anything and everything by making the best and most of it all, come what may.

In the course of living my life for 76 years, I've come to think that nothing happens by pure chance; that there's some force guiding us — call it God, destiny, fate. As soon as a student is ready, a teacher appears, not a moment sooner or not a moment later, like the Zen saying that if you are willing to travel around the world to meet a teacher, one will appear, one has to believe in the perfect harmony of it all.

Our mothers (some of them, at the very least) practiced the so-called 'prenatal education' of us before our birth here on Earth. Perhaps it behooves us to do the same before our birth on another star as our time of sojourning on this planet is running out, alas, willy-nilly! No wonder every moment grows ever more precious to us all, young and old alike.

There is a new word in medical terminology, "didorphine," I'm told, which is said to be 4,000 times more powerful than endorphine. They say this elixir of life/youth is naturally produced in our body when we become children again, playing with our grandchildren.

"For anything to happen anytime anywhere, the whole universe has to conspire." This sentence may be summarized in one word, 'serendipity.' Looking back, everything that occurred before birth and onward seemed to have come about by virtue of serendipity. How else can anyone explain it?

Just as much as translation is creative writing, so is reading, for you only find what you are looking for. Thus we are writing our own life-and-love stories, if not written on paper, then engraved in our hearts, for others as well as our offspring. Success stories show all the possibilities while tales of failure teach us how to rise like a phoenix from its ashes. So there is nothing to be discarded.

Pop icon, singer and now philanthropist Lady Gaga was quoted as saying: "One of the things I hope to impress upon everyone is that all it takes is just one person to belive in you." That 'one person' is yourself, she must have implied. That is one's confidence in one's self and one's peacefulness with one's self, namely one's self-sufficiency. José Mujica, the former guerrilla who is Uruguay's President, living in a run-down house on Montevideo's outskirts with no servants at all and with two plainclothes officers parked on a dirt road as his security detail, says, quoting the Roman court-philosopher Seneca: "It is not the man who has too little, but the man who craves more, who is poor."

American Nobel Prize winning physicist Steven Weinberg wrote in his 1977 book *The First Three Minutes*: "The more the universe seems comprehensible, the more it also seems pointless." By this statement, he must have meant we have to make our points by how we live and love for the universe to acquire meaning. We can take a hint from a truism that 'a traveler's writings say more about the traveler than about the place traveled to.'

Or it may be as Mark Twain says in his farewell address: "Narrative should flow as flows the brook. . .a brook that never goes straight for a minute. . . . Nothing to do but make the trip; how of it is not important so that the trip is made."

No matter where one is from, whether from the East, the West, the North or the South, it doesn't matter. If we look at things from the big picture, we all are 'cosmians' passing through as fleeting sojourners on this tiny planet earth in the sea of cosmos. This is the whole point I wanted to make, just to remind ourselves of the Cosmos Cantata we've got to sing all together.

If each one of us is indeed a micro-cosmos reflecting a macro-cosmos, all that existed in the past, all that exists at present and all that will exist in the future, we're all in it together, all on our separate journeys to realize this.

May each one of us be the sea of cosmos!

"I saw a child carrying a light.
I asked him where he had brought it from.

He put it out, and said:
'Now you tell me where it is gone.' "
—Hasan of Basra